SCHIRMER'S LIBRARY
OF MUSICAL CLASSICS

Vol. 2052

DMITRI KABALEVSKY

Piano Concerto No. 3, Op. 50
"Youth Concerto"

For Piano and Orchestra

Revised Edition by Marcel G. Frank

ISBN 978-0-634-07898-9

G. SCHIRMER, *Inc.*

DISTRIBUTED BY

HAL•LEONARD®
CORPORATION
7777 W BLUEMOUND RD PO BOX 13819 MILWAUKEE WI 53213

Dmitri Kabalevsky (1904-1987)

———

Dmitri Kabalevsky was born in St. Petersburg, Russia on December 30, 1904. He received a liberal education from his father; as a boy, Dmitri excelled in the arts. He wrote poetry and painted, in addition to being an aspiring pianist. However, not unlike other parents of artists at the time, Kabalevsky's father wished him to pursue a career outside of the arts. In 1922, Kabalevsky took the entrance exam to the Engels Socio-Economic Science Institute, where he would likely pursue a career in mathematics or economics, like his father. Young Dmitri never enrolled in the school, however, and was determined to pursue a career in music. He studied and taught piano at the Scriabin Institute, where he composed works for his students, establishing a lifelong interest in providing young musicians with quality literature. In 1925, Kabalevsky went to the Moscow Conservatory to continue studies in piano and composition. While there, he composed the first works to be recognized internationally: the Piano Concerto No. 1 (1928), and the Sonatina in C major (1930) for piano. He eventually became a full professor at the Moscow Conservatory in 1939.

Kabalevsky had a successful career as a composer in the USSR due to a conservative aesthetic temperament, avoiding the difficulties encountered by his contemporaries Sergei Prokofiev and Dmitri Shostakovich, while still producing a large body of fresh and original music. Even so, following the 1948 party decree on music in the Soviet Union, Kabalevsky's works became significantly more lyrical in quality. It was during this period that he composed three concertos for young performers, including works for violin (1948), violoncello (1948-9) and the Concerto No. 3 for Piano (1952). His later pieces include many large works for chorus and orchestra, for which he remains most known in his native country. His orchestral works, concertos, and particularly his piano music brought him notoriety in the United States. Kabalevsky died in Moscow on February 18, 1987.

The **PIANO CONCERTO NO. 3,** Op. 50, nicknamed the "Youth Concerto," is sunny and tuneful, as are all three student concertos. The Piano Concerto No. 3 harkens back to the spirit of the great concertos of Tchaikovsky and Rachmaninoff, with expansive romantic melodies and keyboard pyrotechnics, although within a student capability. Kabalevsky dedictated this and the other two concertos for young performers to the Soviet youth.

PIANO CONCERTO NO. 3
("Youth Concerto")

Revised Edition by
Marcel G. Frank

Dmitri Kabalevsky
(1904-1987)

Poco più mosso ♩ = 152

Poco più mosso ♩ = 152

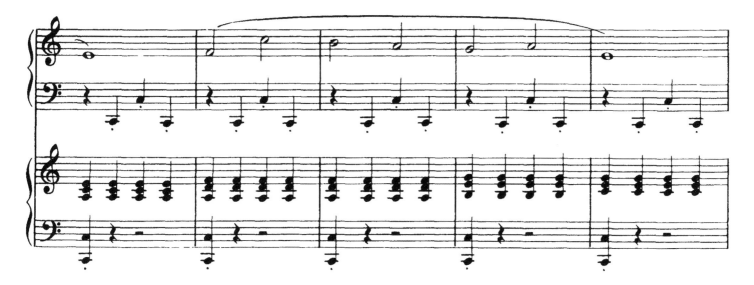

14

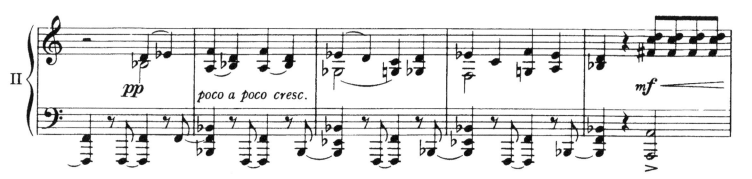

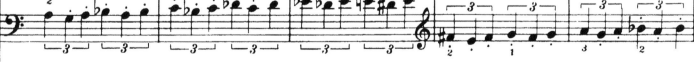

(poco sost.)

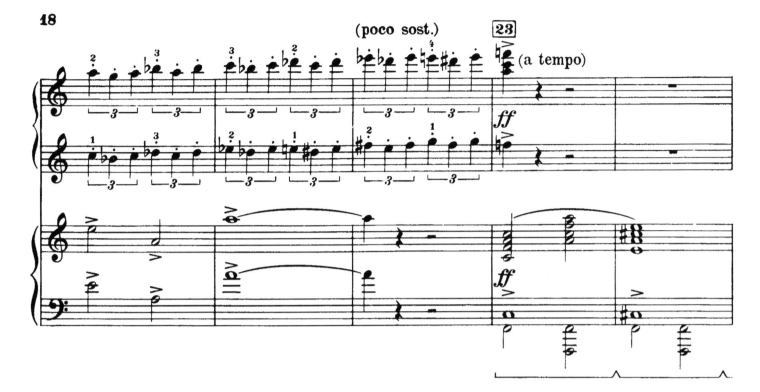

(a tempo)

poco allargando

CADENZA

poco a poco accelerando

Allegro molto

poco a poco cresc.

24

II

Andante con moto ♩ = 72

Ancora pochissimo più mosso ♩. = 104

Ancora pochissimo più mosso ♩. = 104

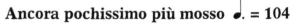

poco accel.

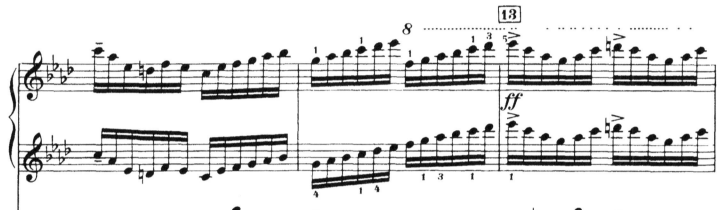

poco ritenuto

Tempo I

(sostenuto)

III

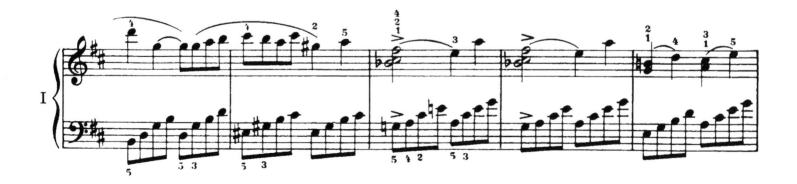

poco allargando   **Poco sostenuto**

Poco sostenuto

16 Marciale (ben ritmico)

Marciale (ben ritmico)

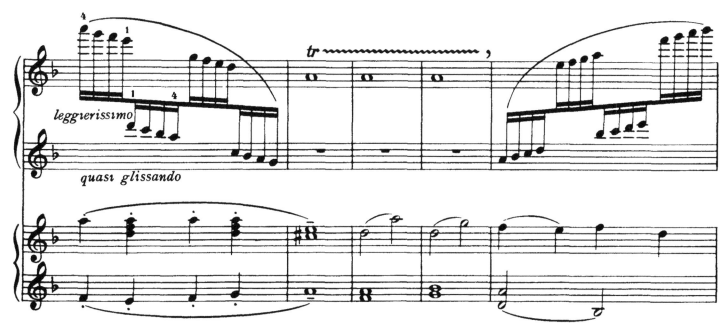

poco a poco allargando

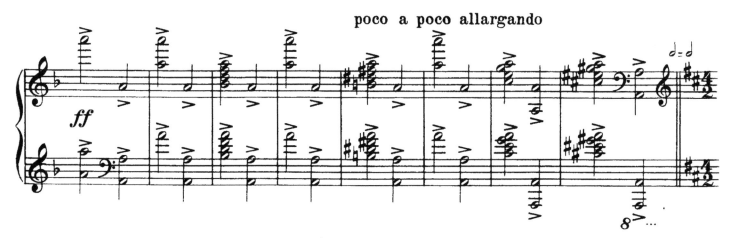

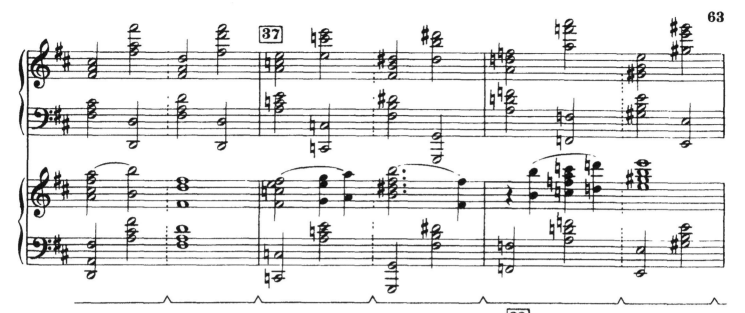

poco allargando

poco allargando